Cape Ann and
Beyond the Cut Bridge

Cape Ann and Beyond the Cut Bridge

Culling and Cart-wheeling

Sharon R. Chace

RESOURCE *Publications* • Eugene, Oregon

CAPE ANN AND BEYOND THE CUT BRIDGE
Culling and Cart-wheeling

Copyright © 2015 Sharon R. Chace. All rights reserved. Except for brief quotations in critical publications or reviews, no part of this book may be reproduced in any manner without prior written permission from the publisher. Write: Permissions. Wipf and Stock Publishers, 199 W. 8th Ave., Suite 3, Eugene, OR 97401.

Resource Publications
An Imprint of Wipf and Stock Publishers
199 W. 8th Ave., Suite 3
Eugene, OR 97401

www.wipfandstock.com

ISBN 13: 978-1-61097-878-1

Manufactured in the U.S.A.   07/13/2015

Dedicated to the Meriden Poetry Society of Connecticut
and The Rockport Poetry Readers of Cape Ann

Contents

Acknowledgments   *xi*

Introduction   *xiii*

Beauty as Revelation:
An Essay of Context   *xxix*

Culling Cape Ann

Angling	3
Hometown Run	4
Situated	5
Tracking	6
A Pet's Passing	7
Kitty	8
Etheree of Time	9
Overcast	10
Writing Life	11
Fulfillment	12
Green Stamp	13
New Englander I Am	15
Deed to the Future	16
Ten Telling Syllables	17
Winter 2008	19
Hearth of Good Will	20
Pitch	21
Rockport Trio-let	22
Rockport Quatrains	23
Petite Ode to Pigeon Cove	24

CONTENTS

Basic Colors	25
Infusion	26
Nor'easter	27
Masked Desire	28
Etheree of Tides	29
Rockport Town Meeting	30
Uncertain Forecast	31
Dumpster Divers	32
Freebie	33
History Lesson	34
Library Trio-let and Library Trio-let 2	35
For John Ronan	36
Sky Queens (under construction) and Sky Queens (constructed)	37
Holy Hopefulness	38
Art Class Sonnet	39
Variations on Motif No. 1	40
Poet Reporting	41
Sonnet of Faith	42
Advent Waiting	43
Christmas Tree Sonnet	44
Feeding	45
Glossary of Glory	46
Haiku of Onshore Wind	47
Cloudy Beach Day	48
Seven Word Conjuring	49
Dead Whale	50
Summer	51
Legacy of Good Harbor	52
Magnification	53
Sonnet for Sailors	55
Cycle Sonnet and P.S.	56
Star Peace	57
Seasoning	58
September Lift	59
Onward and Upward	60

CONTENTS

Cart-wheeling Across the Cut Bridge

Cart-wheeling	63
Albion Haiku	65
Bird Call	66
Horizons	67
Page Turner	68
Well Worn	69
To Walpole with Love	70
A Love Trio-let	71
Etheree of Meriden Poetry Society	72
Punctuation	73
Painting Poems	74
A Haiku of Mighty Morning	76
Spring Trio-let	77
Postcard from Michigan	79
Haiku Trilogy	80
Plant Life	81
Found Poem	83
Yosemite in Haiku Notes	84
A Ghazal Celebrating Elder Men	85
Across the Continent	87
Japanese Gardens	88
Painted Hills	89
Blanket of Many Colors	91
East-West Ridges	94
A Cat and a Jesuit	95
Tilt-turn Windows	96
Winged Warrior	97
Greetings	98
Radiance	99
Butterflies Braiding	100

Epilogue   101

Bibliography   105

Acknowledgments

My thanks to the editors of the following publications, in which previous versions of some of the poems in this book were published.

The Littleton Courier: "A Ghazal Celebrating Elder Men"

Gloucester Daily Times: "Cycle Sonnet and P.S.," "Feeding," "Haiku of Onshore Wind," "Dead Whale," "Etheree of Tides," "History Lesson," "Library Triolet," "Magnification," "Masked Desire," "Nor'easter," "New Englander I Am," "Petite Ode to Pigeon Cove," "Rockport Triolet," "Sky Queens," "Summer," "Town Meeting," and "Winter 2008."

Record Journal: "A Pet's Passing," "Art Class Sonnet," "Cloudy Beach Day," "Deed to the Future," "Greetings," "Hometown Run," "Haiku Trilogy," "Kitty," "Onward and Upward," "Page Turner," "Plant Life," and "Situated."

High Tide (2007), a publication of the Milford, Connecticut, Arts Council: "A Cat and a Jesuit."

Images of Light: Ascent to Trust in Triumph (Resource Publications, 2013): "Radiance."

On Wings of Verse.75th Anniversary Edition, Meriden Poetry Society 2009: "Hometown Run," and "Sonnet for Sailors."

Portfolio of Painterly Poems: A Pilgrim's Path to God (Resource Publications, 2006): "Art Class Sonnet" and "Cloudy Beach Day."

The illustration for "Feeding" was done by Frances McGrath, my friend since childhood, who understands the importance of birds and wildflowers on Cape Ann, in Texas, England, and lands unseen. Thank you, Franny.

Thank you Patricia T. Anders and Karen Barr Grossman for suggestions and assistance with the preparation of this manuscript.

Introduction

THIS BOOK IS ABOUT Cape Ann, Massachusetts, and places in the wider world that have entered my heart. Sometimes place is in my inner world as in the poem "Punctuation," in which pause to rest invites sightings of beauty. "Infusion" is about personal interiors.

The context of the poems is beauty as revelation to poets and others. Revelation or disclosure of meanings that are expressed in poems or other forms of art can be subdivided into celebration, protest or lament, and mystical moments. That which is revealed may be the importance of the ordinary, the spiritual in the profane, a sense of place, humanity run amok, or conversely a glimpse of humanity on tiptoe, or even God in whom we "live and move and have our being." Beauty is found on Cape Ann and in the world beyond our island. Beauty can be friendly and a cause for mystical celebrations, as in pastoral poems about nature. Beauty may also be found in incongruous expressions of pain and lament when suffering touches hearts and flows into words or painterly images. "Plant Life" deals with sin and suffering. There is a hint of prophetic protest in "Winged Warrior" and in "Etheree of Tides."

Readers who have not visited Cape Ann may want to know more about it, especially Rockport, which is my hometown. Situated on the northern point of the cape, Rockport is a small town of less than seven thousand people. We have a board of selectmen and various committees. Please note that the title of "selectmen" is a job description, not a gender designation. Depending upon when you read this book, either most or all of our selectmen will be women! Volunteer fire and ambulance services serve us well. My sister of heart and hearth, Rosemary Lesch, is one of our harbormasters, along with Scott Story. Rosemary's mother, the late Eleanor C. Parsons, brought me up from the age of four along with Rosemary after my first mother, Katharine Rogers Parsons, died. Eleanor was the author of books about Rockport; Katharine was a librarian and artist who worked in oils. Eleanor "Ellie" gave me a love for words; my mother gave me the joy of colors.

INTRODUCTION

Rockport is a popular tourist destination, and the season officially opens with the celebration of "Motif No.1 Day." "Motif No. 1" is an iconic red fish shack, given this name due to its popularity as a subject for artists and photographers over the years.

It took a while, however, for Rockport's famous fish shack to be recognized. In 1932, two Rockporters, Dr. Earl Green and Mr. A. Carl Butman, a businessman, watched the American Legion Convention's parade in Detroit. Inspiration struck and a plan emerged with the goal of promoting Rockport. They decided that a float with a replica of Motif No. 1 should be in the next year's parade in Chicago.

After enlisting talented townspeople from Rockport to build the amazingly realistic float, they entered their "Motif No. 1" into the parade in Chicago a thousand miles away. On their way home right afterwards, bound over roads that must have been as bumpy as the choppy ocean that fisherman navigated, they learned en route that they had won first prize! Reception committees formed back in Rockport to honor the crew and celebrate the victory.

Unfortunately, the blizzard of 1978 destroyed the original shack. But since the director of public works, "Salty" Owens, had the foresight to draw up plans, the building could be rebuilt in its original form after the devastating storm.[1] It is this special fish shack that makes its way into my poems, "Art Class Sonnet" and "Variation on Motif #1."

The three main sections of Rockport are downtown, the south end, and Pigeon Cove, which is also known as the North Village. "Petite Ode to Pigeon Cove" expresses the essence of my days in Pigeon Cove between third and seventh grade. As the tide comes into the natural rock pool at the edge of the ocean, the pool like a bathtub fills up with water. At age eight sitting in the pool soaking in the beauty, I had no idea that in sixty years I would write my favorite Cape Ann poem about it! Readers who find affinity with this poem will enjoy Betty Kielinen Erkkila's book, *My Little Chickadee: Coming of Age in the 1940s & 1950s Rockport, Massachusetts*. Her description of Pigeon Cove lovingly captures a time past.

Like Rockport mothers before me, I took daughter Amy to Front Beach for swimming lessons (the other downtown beach is aptly named "Back Beach"). She provided inspiration for "Cloudy Beach Day" because she told me how much she liked the cloudy days of sweatshirts and more intense salt air. But the love of sweatshirts is not for girls only. In her meditation

---

1. Parsons, *Bearskin Neck: Rockport 1743 to 2005*, 69.

INTRODUCTION

"The Preciousness of Now!" in *Out of the Fog: Meditations for Believers and Skeptics*, Sarah Clark describes a rainy Rockport day when her son Aram and cousins trekked down Bearskin Neck to buy sweatshirts.

Highlights of downtown are the Shalin Liu Performance Center, the Art Association, the Rockport Public Library, and the First Congregational Church that hosts the Old Sloop Coffee House. The church is nicknamed the "Old Sloop" because, like a large ship it is visible from offshore, its steeple guides sailors to the safety of home port.

Crossing over the Annisquam River to the mainland is symbolic of the pull of the world, which lies beyond our stretch of rocky shores. Even as a child I feared I might not get over the cut bridge, which at that time was literal as well as metaphorical. People often ask me why I went to Albion College in Michigan. Well, my attendance at Albion transported me to another viewpoint and provided me with an experience of Midwestern America, expanding ideas about art, and exhilarating academic study of religion. Still, every speech I wrote for a freshman speech class was about Rockport! The professor first thought, "Oh, no. Here she goes again," but told me that every presentation was interesting and enjoyable. I missed the salt air but breathed in the oxygen of fresh study. The poems in the second section of this book, "Cart-wheeling across the Cut Bridge," come from savoring the beauty and challenges of other places. Although I am grateful for the contours of Cape Ann that continue to mold me, expanding matrices beyond the circle of Cape Ann that also shape and sustain me are praise worthy.

Reading Lucy Larcom's 1880 book, *Wild Roses of Cape Ann, and Other Poems*, I realized we have much in common. She is my Cape Ann literary and spiritual ancestor.

Because she lived in Beverly, she would have been described by my paternal grandmother Winifred Parsons as from "off the place." Beverly is about twenty miles south of Rockport, which would have been a day's walk for Lucy. Yet she was very much of the place called Cape Ann, which she visited and absorbed for her soul's sake and her writing.

For most of her life, she was a Congregationalist. I am a member of the First Congregational Church of Rockport, and Larcom's hymn "Draw Thou My Soul, O Christ" is in the *Pilgrim Hymnal*, which we still use. I feel we have a shared spirituality defined as openness to transcendent goodwill revealed in beauty, human friendships, nature, and God. Larcom understood deity in a gentler, more immanent, and fuller aesthetic sense than the Puritan piety of her day. As evidenced in the poem "R.W. E." (May 25, 1880),

INTRODUCTION

Larcom found a breath of fresh air, opening doors, and widening worlds in the thinking of Ralph Waldo Emerson.[2] My sense is that, like me, she had an Emersonian thought process but not many Emersonian conclusions. In "R. W. E.," Larcom acknowledged that Emerson opened doors, stirred sluggish souls, and brought a sense of widening worlds and ample air. Yet she did not completely endorse his ideas. Combining Larcom's diaries and letters with his insightful commentary, Daniel Dulany Addison published *Lucy Larcom Letters, and Diary*, in 1894. From Larcom's diary of 1862, he provides us with the following:

> I heard Ralph Waldo Emerson speak too. "Civilization" was his subject; nobly treated, except that the part of Hamlet was left out of Hamlet. What is civilization without Christianity? There was a kind of religion in what he said; an acknowledging of all those elements which are the result of Christianity; indeed, Emerson's life and character are such as Christianity would shape. He only refuses to call his inspiration by its right name. The source of all great and good thought is in Christ; so I could listen to the Sage of Concord, and recognize the voice of the Master he will not own in words.[3]

Put most simply, God as "Unseen Friend" is more personal that Emerson's divinity as "Over-soul." In a letter of March 14, 1893, to Miss Fobes, whom Larcom met at Monticello Seminary in Illinois, Larcom writes, "Now the best seems to me the simplest:—to receive, and to give by living it, the life of Christ. That is the thought I have kept before me and in my little book, which I call 'The Unseen Friend.'"[4] It seems to me that Larcom must have missed out on the hymn "What a Friend We Have in Jesus," written by Joseph Scriven in 1857. Maybe this hymn that comforted so many, and still continues to do so, did not make it south of Canada into New England Puritan country. Larcom might be happy to know that today in the First Congregational Church of Rockport, a member of the United Church Christ that is open and affirming, we stress hospitality and friendship.

Larcom remained thoroughly Trinitarian and in 1890 was confirmed in the Episcopal Church.[5] She became friends with Phillips Brooks, who is best known for writing the hymn "O Little Town of Bethlehem" and for his pastorate at Trinity Church in Boston. Inspired by Brooks, she wrote

---

2. Larcom, *Wild Roses of Cape Ann and Other Poems*, 175.
3. Addison, *Lucy Larcom: Life, Letters, and Diary*, 125.
4. Ibid., 283.
5. Larcom, *The Poetical Works of Lucy Larcom*, vi.

her book *The Unseen Friend*. Imagining a warmer and friendlier world, she asked, "What is the highest and purest human friendship, but a prophecy of the Friend who is both human and Divine?"[6] Another friend, poet John Greenleaf Whittier, who was a Quaker and Abolitionist, helped Larcom forge with tensile strength her convictions expressed in *The Unseen Friend*. In 1892, Larcom wrote to Whittier about her book project and said that the thought is about seeing him who is invisible. She asked permission to dedicate the book to him and said, "I should like to have one book of mine indicate something of what your friendship has helped me to see and to be."[7] The dedication states,

> To
> John Greenleaf Whittier
> Most Beloved and Most Spiritual of American Poets,
> Whose Friendship Has Been to Me
> Almost A Life-Long Blessing
> I Offer This Little Attempt to Write Upon
> a Great Theme.

The spiritual journey from Puritan to Episcopalian was not without struggle. Rev. Brooks helped her navigate the sacraments and assured Larcom that she need not give up the good things she found in Puritanism such as the high regard for Sabbath rest.[8] Larcom's experience was that the Episcopal Church preached a practical, spiritual life—more than systems and doctrines—through the Christian year, repeating the story and spirit of Christ's life.[9] Larcom also thought that no church is perfect. Although she chose the Episcopal Church as a place where she could most fully live in Christ, she did not see her new church as the only door to Christ. To summarize, she spoke in March 1890 of the many doors of entrance into one vast temple.[10]

As skilled as Larcom was at synthesizing different faith communities, she was not enthusiastic about emerging critical biblical scholarship. In 1882, through her diary she voiced her objections to Renan's *Life of Jesus*. She blames Renan's thought on "some lack of perception in himself." While

---

6. Larcom, *The Unseen Friend*, 36.
7. Shepard, *Letters of Lucy Larcom to the Whittiers*, 517.
8. Addison, 74.
9. Ibid., 284.
10. Ibid., 251.

INTRODUCTION

fascinated with Renan's book, she was strongly annoyed at the thought of Renan's conclusion that the Gospel of John is partially composed of legends and memories transformed by the author of this gospel. She saw his book as based on beautiful yet inadequate concepts.

It is here that Larcom and I part completely harmonious company, because of different understandings about the nature of biblical language. While I believe that God is more than metaphor, human language for talking about God is metaphorical. Ultimately, God is beyond human language. The power of poetic metaphor and the sustenance of symbol is more help for me than literal interpretation in striving to participate in the life of Christ. Of course, I must remember that I live in a different century.

Larcom's book *An Idyl of Work* is a 183-page poem that reads like a novel and far more compelling than I expected. Three girls befriend one another in their joys and challenges as workers in the mills in Lowell, Massachusetts. In addition to telling a heart-warming story, Larcom presents theology as autobiographically informed fiction. She describes God as "Heavenly Helper," "Friend Divine," and "All-Loving Heart."[11] She found God near in every kind thought of the human heart.[12] She believed that souls meet more truly in love than in dogma.[13] She thought that God is known in God's gifts and that the "Invisible God" is recognized in all things visible. For Larcom, God was "Friend" and earthly friendships were hints and shadows of God.[14] Larcom's conception of God as "Invisible Guide"[15] is like my feeling that God is often for me an inner editor. In addition to reading required material in college and graduate school, I have had a sense of other books and journals needed to further my writing life. In prayer, I imagine God as a Compassionate Editor who helps me think of many angles. Experiencing God as a Compassionate Editor helps me to understand and evaluate emotions and opinions. Sometimes those feelings are mine and at other times the feelings of other people. This image of God is explained more fully in my book, *Protestant Pulse: Heart Hopes for God*.

Our book titles are similar and reflect roots in the Cape Ann area and the pull of the world beyond. According to Addison, Larcom had plans for a book she did not live to write. It would have been titled *Hither-ward: A*

11. Larcom, *An Idyl of Work*, 83, 152.
12. Ibid., 14.
13. Ibid., 50.
14. Ibid., 64.
15. Larcom, *A New England Girlhood: Outlined from Memory*, 246.

INTRODUCTION

Life-Path Retraced and one chapter would have been called "The Charm of Elsewhere."[16] This chapter title reminded me of my phrase, "Beyond the cut bridge." The tension between rejoicing in ancestral place and exploring widening shores provides the emotional rhythm in Larcom's poem "Horizon" and my poem "Horizons."

Like Larcom, I am rooted north of Boston by the sea, yet am drawn to the mountains of New Hampshire and Maine. On September 5, 1861, Larcom asked, "Why do I not love to be near the sea better than among the mountains? . . . I believe I was born longing after the mountains."[17] In her poem "In a Cloud Rift," she described sitting on the loftiest White Mountain peak (I'm assuming she meant Mount Washington) in silence eloquent for God's presence.

Ocean dangers seem ever present in Larcom's outlook, although mountains can be dangerous but not as constantly threatening. Larcom expressed strong contrast in her poem "From the Hills," where she described the hills as religion and the sea as "doubt's unanswered moan to thee."[18] There is incongruous beauty in Larcom's crisp thought in well-honed words that bleed grief from lives lost at sea in "Rafe's Chasm" and "At Georges."

Lucy Larcom is most famous for her book *A New England Girlhood: Outlined from Memory*, republished by Northeastern University Press in 1986. This classic book is about her role as a textile worker, her friendships, memories of place, and the literary papers that she and other young women produced. She was sixty-five when she wrote about her girlhood days. No wonder in her poem "October," she states that Septembers promise more than they can deliver and that "our latest years may be our best."[19] Likewise, my senior citizen days are my best writing years. She also stated in *A New England Girlhood* that her most natural expression was in poetry.[20] In her letter to Phillips Brooks dated January 17, 1893, Larcom wrote, "I can truly say that the last ten years of my life have been better and happier than all that went before."[21] My last years here in Rockport are also my most productive and happy.

16. Addison, iv.
17. Addison, 100.
18. Larcom, *Wild Roses of Cape Ann*, 159.
19. Larcom, *Wild Roses of Cape Ann*, 125.
20. Larcom, *A New England Girlhood*, 8.
21. Addison, 286.

INTRODUCTION

Larcom had another late-in-life accomplishment that blossomed from her earlier experiences. In 1846, at the age of twenty-two, she moved with her sister Emeline and Emeline's husband to Illinois. Larcom taught school and then enrolled in Monticello Female Seminary in Godfrey, Illinois. She graduated in 1852 and went on to teach in Wheaton Seminary, now Wheaton College, in Norton, Massachusetts. She continued to write. Wheaton alumna, United Church of Christ minister and member of First Congregational Church of Rockport, the Reverend Dr. Elizabeth Rice-Smith and I shared many conversations and e-mails. In summary, she says:

> The legacy of Lucy Larcom is enduring. Her legacy continues to matter because her writings about her life, her faith, and her interests in nineteenth-century labor issues make her accessible to girls and women today. She inspires her readers through her character and activities. I became aware of Lucy Larcom's presence on the North Shore as a girl growing up in Central Massachusetts, and then was delighted as an undergraduate student majoring in Religion, living in Larcom, to discover that the dormitory was named after her at Wheaton College in Norton, Massachusetts! Sharon Chace enlivens Lucy Larcom for us here on Cape Ann, and for readers throughout the world.

For Lucy Larcom and for me, beauty is revelatory. Addison noted Larcom's poetic hermeneutic:

> Poetry, to her, was vastly more than word-shaping, or combinations of accented and unaccented syllables; it was an attitude of mind and soul towards all existence, a view-point of her being, from which she saw such visions, and heard such sounds, that the impulse was irresistible to record in recognized poetic form her ideas and feelings. She found poetry in everything around her; it was the atmosphere she breathed, the medium, like imponderable ether, through which she saw life. Nature had a more profound meaning to her than the charm of color, or the changing pleasures of the land or the sea. It was the visible evidence of the unseen, the prophecy of a greater fulfillment, the proclamation of the spiritual element within, which the senses of themselves could not perceive. She once said, "Nature is one vast metaphor through which spiritual truth may be read:"—
>
> > "The Universe is one great loving Thought,
> > Written in Hieroglyphs of bud and bloom."[22]

---

22. Addison, 195.

INTRODUCTION

In her poem "A Strip of Blue," Larcom wrote: "Thy universe, O God, is home, / In height or depth, to me; / Yet here upon thy footstool green/ Content am I to be; / Glad when is opened unto my need/Some sea-like glimpse of Thee."[23] Looking at a world in snow, Larcom wrote: "A new earth, bride of a new heaven, / Has been revealed to me."[24] In her poem "One Butterfly," Lucy wrote about seeing colors hidden by sunshine yet revealed by shadows of clouds: "To read that revelation / There's none save thou and I, / In all this noon-lit silence, / My white-winged butterfly."[25]

I also have written about white butterflies in my poem, "Butterflies Braiding." Over the years, white butterflies have given me delight and assurance of friendly beauty and even ongoing life beyond earthly existence. After my father-in-law's graveside service, my husband, Ernest, and I stopped on the way back to Rockport from Mansfield, Massachusetts, at what must have been one of the last Howard Johnson restaurants. I seldom drink soda, or as older Rockporters say "tonic," but that day I had a Coca-Cola. The restaurant was crowded, so we sipped our sweet drinks outside in the warm sunshine. A white butterfly landed on my cheek and stayed so long, it was as if he had something to say.

Color played an important part in Larcom's spiritual life, as it does in mine. She told Whittier that she saw the original painting of "Dante and Beatrice" by Schoeffer at the Athenaeum. While she preferred the engraving to the colorful painting, she added that there would be much of the beauty of colors in the hereafter to make us glad. She believed that the soul sees the subtlest shades of beauty, and that in the hereafter the soul's eyes will be fully open.

Oh, dear Lucy, I wish I could tell you about March 6, 2014. So in my imagination, I will speak to you. My husband Ernie and I went to the Haverhill Public Library so that I could read your letters to the Whittiers. That morning your poetry was mentioned by poet John Ronan, former Gloucester poet laureate, in the *Gloucester Daily Times*. The sun was shining and warmed our faces as we rode in our Prius, a vehicle that would be hard for you to imagine—a horseless carriage that runs partly by gasoline and partly by electricity. Most trolley-trains have disappeared. The Merrimack River that sustained you during you working days at the mill was a

---

23. Larcom, *Wild Roses of Cape Ann*, 43.
24. Larcom, *Wild Roses of Cape Ann*, 131.
25. Ibid., 140.

perfect shade of sapphire. I thought of the harebells you found on its banks, and remembered your sense of sacramental beauty in flowers.

Jennifer, the librarian in charge of the Whittier collection, was a bit worried about finding your letters even with a call number. She opened the locked case and put her hand right on it—a booklet so tiny it would have been very hard to spot. I was so happy to find your words about colors and your hope for the presence of colors in the hereafter. I have speculated about the presence of color beyond earthly life in my poem "Blue Sonnet." This poem, and my watercolor/collage abstract painting with the same name, is based on an experience of God in Exodus 24:9–15 when the elders/fathers of Israel went up the mountain and saw under the feet of God a sapphire pavement. My collage was used on the cover of my book, *Portfolio of Painterly Poems: A Pilgrim's Path to God*. There is a red dot in the painting. Although God is not a red dot, this red dot is a focal point, and God can be a focal point.

Another poem, "Indigo Bunting Sonnet," presents data to support the possibility that my second mother communicated to me from beyond. Both poems have been in my other books, yet must be repeated now for new readers. I share them with you. Like you, I sense mystery in beauty. Thank you for your words: "The secrets of beauty in God's universe." That thought converges with my words, "temporal ambiguity" and "beauty's mystery" in "Indigo Bunting Sonnet."

Blue Sonnet

Blue morning glories reach from ground to sky,
Jacob's ladder connecting earth, heaven.
Singing, angel muse patiently stands by.
Pure hue, glory, loveliness is leaven.
Hagar looking upon the face of God
Lived. So shall those whose gaze is strong enough
To embrace the icon nourished in sod.
Beauty so deep sadness is joyful hush.
Fathers of Israel saw beneath God's feet
A sapphire pavement. Hallow, praise, chant.
Sing in Heaven's City evil's defeat.
Foundations of treasured, precious blue stone,
Power, purest presence, God's face alone.

INTRODUCTION

Indigo Bunting Sonnet

Two weeks before Eleanor Parsons died
I asked her for a sign from the Beyond
Specifying two indigo buntings
Loveliest birds, pure notes of heaven's song.
Two birds don't have to be in the same place.
Just one would seem like a coincidence.
Double sightings would make a stronger case,
Confirm God's wide welcome, love's deepest sense.
Before the memorial service day
A blessed sympathy note came in the mail
An indigo bunting: "Thank you." I prayed.
Bunting also on the back, my spirit sailed.
Proof or temporal ambiguity
Creating room for beauty's mystery?

Lucy, our shared affinity for blue and yellow amazes me. On the back cover of my most recent book, *Images of Light: Ascent to Trust in Triumph*, Donna Schaper, senior minister at Judson Memorial Church in New York City, said: "Color is the way this writer gets to God. She loves yellow sometimes more than blue, blue sometimes more than yellow, and art as much as God. Read this book and you will find your way toward much color, art, and even a little God." Color and art convey God and Christ to me. I just told our newly settled minister, the Rev. Derek van Gulden, that if the time comes when I can no longer go to Easter services, I will enter into the joy of the resurrection by holding in my mind the golden-yellow globe behind the resurrected Christ in Matthias Grünewald's painting "Resurrection." To my mind, that gold orb is both an artistic and religious achievement.

Lucy, I cherish your poem, "Golden Rod." Comparing the heavenly blue harebell with sun-like gold of golden-rod, you said you did not know which one most delighted you. My sense is that by the end of the poem, you chose goldenrod because, through the sun-shaped blossoms, souls receive the light of God and give back the glow. I note with delight that you gave Whittier, who loved bright yellows, a blue vase to hold yellow flowers.[26]

---

26. Marchalonis, *The worlds of Lucy Larcom*, 132.

INTRODUCTION

I hope my book inspires readers, especially those of us who live north of Boston, to read your poems. "Rafe's Chasm" expresses tragedy in such a beautiful way that readers can take it in and reflect. What a gift to Cape Ann! Your "Mistress Hale of Beverly" is a brilliant distillation of the witch trials. Poetry as a form of history can invite readers to enter into the heart and soul as well as the facts. I think of "John Brown's Body" by Stephen Vincent Benet. I think that your poem in honor of John Greenleaf Whittier, "J.G.W. December 17, 1877," could be used to introduce his poems.

Lucy, you were in good company, and company extends beyond your time. Your perspective on marriage and how it could sap the strength from women is something for many to consider even today. "Sylvia" could be used as a discussion starter in a group of women struggling with the demands of marriage. Rockport harbormasters Rosemary Lesch and Scott Story will appreciate your high regard for working boats in "A Passing Sail." Your poem "Mountaineer's Prayer," asking for the strength of the steadfast hills, will resonate with humanists and people of many faith traditions.

Lucy, as you know, the timing of my trip to Haverhill was serendipitous. Recently, I found an important book, *The worlds of Lucy Larcom 1824–1893*, by Shirley Marchalonis. This discovery was fortuitous. An article, "*From survival to love*" by Bethany Sollereder in *The Christian Century*, issue of September 17, 2014, added to my understanding of Marchalonis's assessment of your poem, "Rose Enthroned." *The Christian Century* is a biweekly journal that emphasizes thinking critically and living faithfully. I fancy that you and Phillips Brooks would find it compelling if you lived today.

To reiterate slightly, Shirley Marchalonis alerted me to the importance of "The Rose Enthroned." In your poem, you describe the cataclysmic geological and botanical forces that formed the world. Chaos subsides. Beauty emerges. Finally, a rose appears that symbolizes beauty and love. You conclude that in time a new flower will make even the rose seem like "A fair and fragile weed." To my mind, in this poem, your brilliance is not masked by piety. Marchalonis wrote that your poem published in the *Atlantic* brought prestige.[27] I think your poem will appeal to both theists and humanists.

I believe that your poem foreshadows the thought of Andrew Elphinstone (1918–1975) who came to my attention in Bethany Sollereder's article in *The Christian Century*. Sollerder reports that *Freedom, Suffering and Love*, a book published after Elphinstone's death was based upon his notes. In response to the problem of suffering, he saw pain as part of evolution.

---

27. Marchalonis, *The worlds of Lucy Larcom*, 139.

INTRODUCTION

Like you, he saw the world as shaped by cataclysmic forces including volcanoes and earthquakes. In his view, spiritual development is similar. At first, our non-human ancestors fought for survival. Chaos and violence ruled. Finally, love emerges. Forgiveness is the ultimate defeat of evil in Sollereder's Christology. Summing up his thought, Sollereder said that Elphinstone shows us how the evolutionary narrative works with the story of Christian redemption. The existence of hatred and violence in the world is part of a process still in development. "The bitter raw products of evolution are slowly being brought to transcend evolution itself. We are, through the painful process of forgiveness, being transformed into the image and likeness of Christ."[28]

Lucy, in my sense of things, love and forgiveness abounding is like your vision of a flower that is even more beautiful than a rose. I applaud your foreshadowing and convergence of thought with Sollereder. Still, I stress that forgiveness and love are not exclusive to Christianity.

I close with hope for blue, gold, and everlasting Light.

As ever,

Sharon

Unfolding the arch of beauty as revelation, Larcom and I both depict themes of inner life, ascent, and images of God. Larcom's poem "Indwelling"[29] and my "Infusion" are both about revelation of God, who is friendly, dwelling in personal interiors. John Bunyan's *Pilgrim's Progress*, which was Larcom's first favorite book, [30] inevitably affects Puritans of Larcom's time and mine. Ever since singing "Climb Every Mountain" at my 1962 Rockport High School graduation, I have felt an underlying sense of ascent. Likewise, Larcom liked what she called the "climbing and flying hymns."[31] My previous book, *Images of Light: Ascent to Trust in Triumph*, is built on this ascent theme. In Lucy Larcom's poem "White Everlasting Flowers," she describes a morning on an unnamed mountain in West Ossippee, New Hampshire, in September 1875. (Like me, she sometimes dated her poems and at other times does not). She advises: "Climb for the white flower of thy dream, / O

28. Sollerder, *From survival to love*, 25.
29. Larcom, *Wild Roses of Cape Ann*, 221–22.
30. Larcom, *A New England Girlhood*, 101.
31. Larcom, *A New England Girlhood*, 68.

pilgrim! let the vision gleam/ As hope and possibility."[32] In my interpretation of her poem "Need and Wish," Larcom saw yearnings as an invitation to strive: "By this path climbs the soul forever."[33] In her poem "Christ the Light," in order to make life complete, she asks, "Help us upward still to strive." Christ is named "Light supreme" and "Life Divine!"[34] Larcom even suggests that the poet reflects the voice of God: "The voice that unto poet and sage / Whispered of God at hand, unknown, / Hath written itself on history's page, / Speaks in a language like our own."[35]

Lucy Larcom is my historical friend and good company across the centuries. In my book *Protestant Pulse: Heart Hopes for God*, I shared my imagined images of God that are metaphors derived from biblical passages. One metaphorical image is God as Poet-Prophet. Neither Larcom's imagination nor mine need to be considered suspect. I believe in John Keats's thought, "that we are compelled to imagine more than we can know or understand."[36] In summary, Phillips Brooks believed that the poet could imagine and picture the fuller life in God, that any person can enter into and find forgiveness.[37] Roland Bainton said that Martin Luther "verged on saying that an excessive emotional sensitivity is a mode of revelation."[38] As I also note in the following chapter, Friedrich Schleiermacher located God in the feeling of absolute dependence. He believed that the imagination is the primary faculty for intuiting the divine.[39] Therefore, there is testimony to the possibility that imagination is a mode of perception or even revelation.

Larcom wrote poems and prose about the wildflowers of her day that included columbine, gentians, barberries, marsh rosemary, beach peas, and harebells. She viewed wildflowers as "the sweetness of this mortal life."[40] Since some wild plants have disappeared, I have to imagine in *Rockport Quatrains* the harebells that I do not remember blooming in the woods of Pigeon Cove. With pride, I tell you that Rockporters, many of whom

---

32. Larcom, *Wild Roses of Cape Ann*, 144.
33. Larcom, *Wild Roses of Cape Ann*, 194.
34. Ibid., 226–27.
35. Ibid., 217.
36. Bloom, *The Best Poems of the English Language: From Chaucer through Frost*, 458–59.
37. Brooks, *Phillips Brooks' Addresses*, 112–13.
38 Bainton, *Here I Stand: A Life of Martin Luther*, 283.
39. Heller, *Reluctant Partners: Art and Religion in Dialogue*, 34.
40. Larcom, *A New England Girlhood*, 216.

INTRODUCTION

are members of the Rockport Garden Club, are working to rid the area of invasive plants that destroy the native ones. Nan Blue, however, wrote a poem addressing these pests in which she had to admit: "Can't call you 'interloper'; you were invited. Didn't crash the party, you came as a guest." The once invited plants are no longer welcomed, but native species are wished a happy return. I was pleased to hear from Nan that they're "working on a plan to reintroduce plantings in groups, including harebells." With great joy, I look forward to the return of harebells on Cape Ann that Larcom loved in the nineteenth century.

Lucy Larcom considered her readers as friends not critics. Following her example: Thank you my readers and friends.

Sincerely,
Sharon
2014

Beauty as Revelation
An Essay of Context

*Beauty in nature, art, and community can be revelatory
of God and transcendent meanings.*

My first experience of revelatory beauty occurred when I was three years old. My first mother, Katharine Rogers Parsons, was dying of leukemia. Light filtered through cobalt blue vases on the windowsill and gave me comfort. Beauty mattered and settled within. Color spoke as a parable of grace. Even though my mother was very ill, she colored with me. My favorite color was blue.

Truth also started to matter. Following the conventional wisdom of the day, my father did not want anyone talking with me about death. However, the minister of the Universalist Church in Gloucester visited the playgroup in his church and did talk with me about my mother's illness. Although I do not recall the exact conversation, I can still remember playing with blocks as we talked. Beauty and truth are building blocks of theological aesthetics.

Most likely, you also have experienced God in beauty. Let us consider beauty in nature, the arts, and community.

Beauty in Nature

People often speak of finding God in nature. Nature can be quieting and consoling. There is biblical precedent for sensing God in nature or the possibility that God is revealed in creation. It is written: "Ever since the creation of the world his eternal power and divine nature, invisible though they are, have been understood and seen through the things he has made" (Rom 1:20). While for years I have not been completely comfortable with the concept of God in nature because nature can be cruel and uncaring, I have, as have countless others, felt the presence of God when pausing in vistas of beauty.

In wrestling with my theological problem, I wrote the following poem that describes beauty as the meeting ground where people meet God and rise beyond themselves.

On Tiptoe

In the darkening of dusk, in the graying of approaching storm,
pink rose of Sharon buds, blue bachelor buttons and orange zinnias
soften the blackening—not by the promise of God in nature—
but through connection on the meeting ground of beauty
that stirs the imagination to envision possibilities beyond the self
when seekers stand on tiptoe to touch Transcendence.

Imagination, as I discussed in my introduction, may help people picture a better and more beautiful world, and even to envision Transcendence, as I did in my poem. Friedrich Schleiermacher located God in "a feeling of absolute dependence." He sensed God in the sublime much like theologian Rudolf Otto's description of the "numinous," and thought that the imagination is the primary faculty for intuiting the divine.[41] Both Schleiermacher and Otto reached beyond the purely rational emphasis of the Enlightenment and located God in mystery. Imagination may enhance the ability to express the numinous and mysterious ways of God and grace.

Sometimes nature and grace come together and, through beauty, lift human hearts. I wrote the following poem during our days in Meriden, Connecticut.

---

41. Heller, *Reluctant Partners: Art and Religion in Dialogue*, 33–34.

BEAUTY AS REVELATION

April Blessing

Robin in the snow,
I wonder if you know
the joy you bring
when you sing of spring?
Pecking through the
crusty ice, you evoke
in me fresh zest for life.
When nature and grace
converge . . .
Beauty is the Word.

People do not need to be believers to feel uplifted in the presence of beauty. Patrick Sherry wrote that perhaps the leading exponent of a revelatory view of beauty in the twentieth century was Simone Weil, French philosopher, political activist, and Christian mystic. She thought of beauty as an experience of the transcendent; more specifically, an experience of God; that for unbelievers, beauty is a form of what she called the implicit love of God. Like Jesus who came to understand that his mission extended beyond Israel, Weil saw God's love for all people. In her description of the world's beauty, beauty is "the sign of love between the Creator and creation."[42] One does not need to be a theist to experience beauty and a spiritual dimension in nature or in art.

My spiritual Puritan ancestor, Jonathan Edwards, linked beauty in nature explicitly with Christ. He thought that when we are delighted with flowery meadows, green trees and fields, rivers and murmuring streams, singing birds, and all the other glories of nature, we should see them as "emanations of the sweet benevolence of Jesus Christ" and "shadow of his infinite beauty and loveliness."[43] Edwards's use of the word *shadow* echoes Paul's description of seeing in a mirror dimly, but in time face to face (1 Cor 13:12). In Edwards's view, God is not only beautiful but also the source of beauty. Edwards is concerned with spiritual beauty and the figure of Christ as revealing absolute beauty. For Edwards, beauty in human nature is "an unrestricted benevolence of a generous heart" that flows into good will.[44]

---

42. Sherry, *Spirit and Beauty: An Introduction to Theological Aesthetics*, 51.

43. Sherry, 14.

44. Farley, *Faith and Beauty: A Theological Aesthetic*, 45.

BEAUTY AS REVELATION

Beauty in the Arts

The biblical precedent for beauty in the arts is tangential. There is attention to the architecture of King Solomon's temple. More significantly to me is the constant repetition of the colors of liturgical vestments in the Hebrew Scriptures (blue, purple, and scarlet). Colors are important for many kinds of artists, and as you have seen for Lucy Larcom and for me. Most likely, you have favorite colors in nature or in art that speak to you and give joy or sustenance.

Sister Wendy Beckett wrote about beauty that enables the viewer to see beyond self. In her book, *Sister Wendy's Odyssey: A Journey of Artistic Discovery*, she discusses the painting "The Gust of Wind" by Auguste Renoir, which is an oil on canvas owned by the Fitzwilliam Museum in Cambridge, England. In this small painting, that is only 20½ inches by 32½ inches, wind blows through the grasses and fluffy clouds touch the horizon. This painting evokes empathy in me because, having sat in a similar field in Rockport, I can imagine the warm sunlight and gentle breezes, and thus share in Renoir's morning in 1875! Sister Wendy wrote: "This small, unpretentious picture shows us what the spiritual in art is all about." She believes that Renoir takes us out of our confined egos into a timeless world and that our stay in that timeless place leaves us changed: "It would be futile to try to say precisely how we are changed, but great art can be recognized subjectively by the effect is has on us. We have been enlarged in our being by receiving the blessing of another's [being]."[45]

However change occurs, responding to art can open a person to new perspectives. In his book, *By Way of Response,* Martin E. Marty discussed one of his favorite philosophers, Eugen Rosenstock-Huessy. Rosenstock-Huessy outlined three epochs of learning in the West. First came, "I believe in order to understand." The next conclusion was "I think therefore I am." Finally Rosenstock-Huessy's motto suggested a way to learn. "I respond although I shall be changed."[46] To my mind, one word that came to me in a dream summarizes Marty's on-going application of this motto. The word is *considering*.

It seems to me that if a stance of responding is shared across the divides of cultures and tribes, there are possibilities for societal transformation as well as for personal change. Whether reflecting on art or responding

---

45. Beckett, *Sister Wendy's Odyssey: A Journey of Artistic Discovery*, 34.
46. Marty, *By Way of Response*, 26–27.

to social challenges, such as the need to grow in inclusiveness, one might glimpse fresh sightings. May our watchword be *considering*?

C. S. Lewis may have partially addressed the question of how we are changed with looking at art and looking at nature. He spoke of natural beauty, yet it seems to me that his thoughts apply also to beauty in art. He surmised that we do not want merely to see beauty, but that we want to be united with it, pass into it, receive it into ourselves and become part of it.[47] In his thinking, this union will not happen in earthly time because, for example, "we discern the freshness and purity of morning, but they do not make us fresh and pure."[48] Maybe he was not exactly correct in seemingly limiting the union with a beauty that purifies to a future time. It seems to me that purification can be partially realized in this life and that beauty helps cleanse personal interiors. Perhaps rest in beauty helps the mind to be uncluttered so as to see ourselves and our situations as they are.

The thoughts of Cecilia González-Andrieu help me to wrestle with how beauty can change people's perceptions by evocation of wonder in transforming moments. I am drawing upon her chapter "In Search of Wonder" in her book *Bridge to Wonder: Art as a Gospel of Beauty*. In summary, we need to see with humility if we are to become aware of our pain and then by awakening to wonder, imagine how pain—ours and other people's—can be transformed into ways to turn the world's sadness into joy. She cites the need for other vantage points. One vantage point is to see what is destructive, and another is to see the beauty of all that we need to preserve and redeem. In her thinking, a renewed sense of humility can sometimes reveal our brokenness and need for salvation.[49]

Experiencing the beauty of the Grand Canyon altered my perception in a moment that has remained transformative. Release from sin and from sorrow, which at times can be related, is redeeming. In 1984, my husband Ernest (Ernie) and daughter Amy, age eleven at the time, and I went to the Grand Canyon. In my essay, "Other rocks, Other colors," published in the *Gloucester Daily Times*, I wrote:

> Just outside our log cabin, I sat on a fat cushion of pine needles, looked and contemplated. The Grand Canyon was formed over many eons. Such immense time put people, plans, and me into perspective. I was part of the picture, although a tiny part. I felt no

---

47 Klein, *A Year with C. S. Lewis: Daily Readings from His Classic Works*, 397.
48 Ibid.
49 Gonzalez-Andrieu, *Bridge to Wonder: Art as a Gospel of Beauty*, 37.

one will ever again be able to hassle me for being slow moving or press me into a bigger job in a project than I feel is the right sized part for me.

We saw beauty which settles within and ripens with joy. In a children's story, "Brighty of the Grand Canyon," by Marguerite Henry, the burro is a symbol of a joyous way of life. I bought a tiny, pewter burro and reaffirmed a promise to cherish the joyful moments which come to me when striving is balanced with play which gives life color.

It would have been sinful not to embrace the gifts of perspective, colors, and beauty.

Thirty years later, I note more fully the theological dimension of change in my aesthetic experience by embracing Cecilia Gonzalez-Andrieu's sentence: "In the beauty that delights us or breaks our heart, something is offered and understood, briefly, as wholeness and healing, and that 'something' changes everything."[50] To use Gonzalez-Andrieu's phrase, the natural beauty of the Grand Canyon was a "gospel of beauty" similar to my early childhood sighting of light coming through blue glass as a parable of grace. Often when I see artwork inspired by the Grand Canyon area, the paintings or photographs also import "a gospel of beauty."

Simone Weil, who also believed that art helps people see beyond themselves, found holiness radiating from Gregorian chant. Pursuing that line of thought, she said that "contact with the beautiful is in the full sense of the term a sacrament."[51] In a similar line of thought, Lucy Larcom, whom you met in my introduction, wrote: "From every wild flower of the field we may drink as from a sacramental chalice overflowing with His love."[52] If beauty as a sacrament seems like a stretch, consider beauty as sacramental. Experiencing beauty as sacramental is a blessing. The following poem illustrates blessings in sacramental beauty.

---

50. Gonzalez-Andrieu, 37.

51. Dunaway and Springsted, *The Beauty That Saves: Essays on Aesthetics and Language in Simone Weil*, 131.

52. Larcom, *The Unseen Friend*, 166.

Summer

Canopy of rose of Sharon,
With music, gift of bees,
Mountains of hydrangea blues,
Blessings for the pleased,
Sunset glow on earth below
Holds and molds receiving souls
On the going, on the way,
Of unfolding day, each day.

Beauty in Community

Life in community can be beautiful. The first verse of Psalm 133 suggests beauty in faith families as well as in biological families: "How very good and pleasant it is when kindred live together in unity!"

In Matthew's story of the anointing at Bethany, an unnamed woman poured a very costly ointment onto Jesus' head (Matt 26:6–13). The disciples were annoyed. In summary, they questioned the waste when the ointment could have been sold and the money given to the poor. The disciples had a point. But Jesus knew that anger may have been at the root of their question and said that the woman had done a good thing for him. The Revised Standard Version states, "For she has done a beautiful thing to me" (Matt 26:10). In the same verse, the New Revised Standard version says, "She has performed a good service for me."

New Testament Greek is a highly nuanced language. There can be many translations for words, and the backgrounds of words have multiple layers. The New Testament word *kalos* can mean good, right, proper, fitting, better, honorable, honest, fine, beautiful, or precious. Both translations of *kalos* as beautiful and as good, when considered together, show the interconnection of goodness and beauty in Christian service.

Service is clearly bent toward justice. In more subtle ways, justice underlies the beauty in art, like a rough sketch guiding the artist's application of paint. Consider the pondering of Saint Augustine who found beauty in balance and proportion: "When I looked at things, it struck me that there was a difference between the beauty of an object considered by itself as one whole and the beauty to be found in a proper proportion between separate things, such as the due balance between the whole of the body and any of its limbs."[53] This classical, symmetrical balance, translated into spiritual thought, connotes the idea of equality in the sight of God or a more balanced distribution of the world's materials. Asymmetrical balance also has spiritual dimensions and implications. To achieve asymmetrical balance, artists have to experiment with arranging the parts. So also it is necessary to think creatively about all the parts, all the issues that need to come together to create a just world. When you create a work of art, know that underneath is a form of balance that can be subliminally experienced as a symbol for fairness, a restored garden of justice, a renewal of humanity dwelling in Eden's beauty. In a not completely dissimilar way, writers, perhaps especially poets, also employ balance. Words and phrases, rhythms and cadence, and spacing in poetry can suggest balance.

St. Augustine and poet Marianne Moore helped me understand Matisse whose art I find comforting and beautiful. Matisse said: "All art worthy of the name is religious."[54] Although I do not know exactly what he meant by that statement, I intuitively agree, and upon further thought about a poem by Marianne Moore and St. Augustine's view of balance, I understand why I concur. In her poem "When I Buy Pictures," Moore imagines buying pictures. Her requirements suggest the spiritual dimension of pictorial art. "It comes to this: of whatever sort it is, it must be 'lit with piercing glances into the life of things'; it must acknowledge the spiritual forces which have made it."[55] Balance that suggests fairness is one spiritual dimension. So also are many kinds of emotional impact, such as the embrace of beauty or conversely of suffering, joy in life or recognition of harsh realities of sin and sorrow. Prophetic critique, celebration, and mystical moments can get to the essences of life.

In addition to the hint that art bends toward justice, belief that art's balance, however achieved, is a whisper that art transcends individual expression. Believing that art and poetry have communal implications can

---

53. Pine-Coffin, *Saint Augustine: Confessions*, 83.
54. O'Roark, "A Beautiful Place," 45.
55. Matthiessen, *The Oxford Book of American Verse*, 751.

safeguard artists and writers from accusing voices claiming that to be an artist or poet is selfish or disconnected from service or from community.

Jesus' sacrificial life and death are the ultimate examples of beauty to the glory of God. Not everyone is called to ultimate sacrifice. Day-to-day sharing as exemplified in the Gospel of Luke can guide both social workers and artists. The beauty of Christ infuses Christian service. Therefore, when you do good things in community for humanity or for God, there is spiritual beauty. According to my study of Gerhard Kittel's *Theological Dictionary of the New Testament*, *kalos*, as it is used in the preaching of the gospel in Matthew, Mark, and Luke, is oriented to the kingdom of God.[56] Believing that beauty in nature, art, and community is part of God's reign, as it is partly realized in the present as well as in the future, can help us affirm the importance of beauty in its many shapes. Embracing beauty is part of what it means to be religious with our sights on God's reign.

---

56. Kittel, *Theological Dictionary of the New Testament Vol. III*, 545.

Culling Cape Ann

Angling

When I was eight, my Father
took me fishing from Granite Pier.
"Only for cunners," he said.
As I recall, you have to be
a bit cunning to catch those
cunners!
Revisiting childhood places,
salt air refreshes. Reflecting
on Rockport, I cast glimpses
of beauty as bait into my mind,
the sea of mystery, the ocean
of hidden treasures.
Cunningly I fish for the
right words, cued by mystery
culled by thought, charged
onward by Cape Ann clues.

Hometown Run

Our good days in Meriden are numbered.
Returning to Rockport on the seacoast,
tiny home we will be less encumbered.

Happy days of joyful writing life merged.
Repressed aspirations—seeds sprouted most.
Our good days in Meriden are numbered.

Harvey the old cat with love softly purrs.
Will he welcome guests and be a good host?
Tiny home we will be less encumbered.

Wood walls, white curtains are blessings incurred.
"Color coordinated cat" we'll boast.
Our good days in Meriden are numbered.

Parting is best yet a stinging of burr.
To on-going life I raise hopeful toast.
Tiny home we will be less encumbered.

Poems emerged that deep in me slumbered.
My word paintings *Record-Journal* did post.
Our good days in Meriden are numbered.
Tiny home we will be less encumbered.

Situated

Upon arrival
the Rose of Sharon tree is
in full bloom—like us.

Harvey is now known
as the cat in the front window
watching his new world.

Flat rock, witness stone,
place to know that God is God,
backyard, holy space.

Tracking

The train that idled overnight
at the end of the line
forty miles north of Boston
fills with commuters who would flower Spring-like
with a little extra money, more sunshine
and margins for their own idling times.

Held in my thoughts for ten years
during our Connecticut days,
I still wonder about their singular stories
tied together with the string of routine,
the tow of rail lines that never converge
and the threads of conversations that do.

A Pet's Passing

Harvey went to his eternal cat nap.
Stoic I am but still greatly saddened.
I dignified him with iambic lines.
The least I can do before telling you
About *Peanut* growing Brazil nut huge.
His coat is blue-gray and his nose is black.
Harvey would approve of this gentle cat.
Inside is safest place. Coyotes roam.
Pets can make Eden and our houses homes.

Kitty

If my cat, *Peanut,* could be a poet,
he would mew in celebration
of running water, flowing streams,
and flowering dogwood in feline dreams.
Content to be a writer's cat,
he purrs, intently—
looking interested in computer calamities,
and piles of papers.
Rescued from the shelter,
he now shelters me with kitty comforts,
interest compounded daily.

Etheree of Time

Time
Has come
To fall in
Love again with
Rockport, my hometown,
Charger plate, nourishment
Sublime, elevation in
Minds feasting on coursing beauty:
Water, rocks, light, Cape Ann elements
Anchored in sacred place transcending space.

Overcast
Homage to Emily Dickinson

Gray days swell wistful in Rockport
when matching inner seascapes.
Sea shells along the shore
sing sweet, swirling music.

Generations gone before
heard the same fine songs
like bits of sand that stick
around and salt the skin.

Rumble, rumble, push and pull
stones drag in undertow.
Seagulls cry and circle round.
Fishing boats are homeward bound.

Ships bend towards Milk Island.
My beat be still.
For harbor rests within my mind.
Might home be found?

Writing Life

Brownies likely . . .
when blessed by friends who come to tea.
Cups of warmth, doily daintiness
lighten aubades and sweeten nocturnes.

When blessed by friends who come to tea,
continuing conversations
lighten aubades and sweeten nocturnes.
Finger foods strengthen hearts for work.

Continuing conversations,
cups of warmth, doily daintiness,
finger foods strengthen hearts for work.
Brownies likely . . .

Fulfillment

Red potatoes in a blue bowl,
one ripe tomato on the kitchen window sill,
peace in the ordinary,
yet happiness is deepened,
thanksgiving heightened
because at last
I am doing work
that makes me glad to be me.

Green Stamp

A hint of April blue
in a February sky,
cirrus clouds feather
a seagull flying by.
I did not intend to rhyme.
The rhyme scheme
came to me: a gift
I may exchange some
day for free verse.
Time will see.

New Englander I Am

I am a New Englander
sustained by the golden
promise of the sacred cod
in the Massachusetts
State House and by the
light of the Boston Public Library.
I am a New Englander
rejoicing in tiny villages
and white steeples,
mountains in fall wearing
back to school colors,
forests featuring
trillium in spring.
I am a New Englander
intoxicated by seaside
sweet peas and wild roses in June.
I am a New Englander
attuned to foghorns that warn.
I am a citizen in community
aligned with beams brightening.
I am a New Englander
believing in lighthouse prisms
beaconing strivers sailing
towards their dreams.
I am a New Englander.

Deed to the Future

Whether excavating an inner lexicon
or sounding the depths of shared sensibilities,
mining the same words, like Emily Dickinson
"I dwell in possibility" and conclude with probability.
Perhaps my style of rhetoric will develop into maverick.
If so, then indeed,
flowers will bloom from liberal seed.

Ten Telling Syllables
Sharon C. Poems

A *Sharon C. Poem* is a poetic form that I invented and named after myself. The form is simple: one line of iambic pentameter aligned vertically.

My name *Sharon* is related to the word *sharing*. It is my hope that people will write these poems and share them with other people.

After writing a sonnet about a memorial bottle tossed overboard in memory of the husband of an elderly friend, I realized that I described the life of a World War II submarine veteran in one line. The line is from "Sonnet for Sailors," which may be found in this book. The line is "Pearl Harbor, submarines, saw Treaty signed."

Then I wondered if other people could express their essences in one line. If people shared ten telling syllables about themselves, all who shared and listened would know others more fully.

Five *Sharon C. Poems* follow.

Rosemary Lesch

Harbor
Ambulance
Safeguarding
Rockport

Roger Lesch

Invites
Navy
Visits
Elders
Protects

Eleanor Parsons

Mother
Writer
Climbing
Courage
Mountain

Ernest Chace

Wildcard
Believing
Quality
Is
Change

Sharon Chace

Painterly
Poet
Protestant
Wildcard

Winter 2008

Inwardly, easterly I sing,
celebrate climate, cooling beauty,
poetically paint New England.
Pink glow on snow
oh! world, you hold me so.
North of Boston land
my soul in work to rest

Hearth of Goodwill

There is something about a full hod of pellets
beside the stove
that signals warmth and love,
well-being and a pleasant life
bending towards generosity
streaming from the spring of gratitude.

Pitch

Rosemary smiled with a mother-in-law's pride
when friends at the Sandy Bay Historical Society
rejoiced in the beauty of daffodils
planted by Bridgit at 25 Granite Street.
"Stay tuned for tulips," she said.

Stay tuned indeed.
Stay tuned for the Memorial Day Parade
with drummers beating in time throughout Time.

Stay tuned for the warm breezes of June
that feel like angels' kisses,
for sand between your toes in August,
for the deepening blue sea in September,
for green gingko leaves turning yellow in front of
the Rockport National Bank.

Stay tuned for the Christmas tree in Dock Square,
for all winter ducks and First Night.
Stay tuned.

Rockport Trio-let

Harbormasters are seaworthy.
Rockport boats rest in the harbor.
Even when winds are easterly.
Harbormasters are seaworthy.
Fog, rocks, waves are gray and pearly.
Ebb and flow feed like a larder.
Harbormasters are seaworthy.
Rockport boats rest in the harbor.

Rockport Quatrains
July 2, 2013

All the pretty sailboats
With spinnakers blooming
Lady slippers of the sea
Brighten fog looming.

To bring back the harebells
Of the 19th century, a dream,
A native plant scene to merge
Mystical blues of sea and of land.

Petite Ode to Pigeon Cove
July 2012

Sunken, magical tide pool
In the rocks of Pigeon Cove
Starfish, seaweed, shadows cool.
Cast in beauty's mold.

Lady slippers, pussy willows, rich dark loam,
In the woods of childhood memory,
Mystery as deep as a Buddhist koan.
Cast in beauty's chemistry.

Indigo buntings perch on telephone wires.
Tool Company turned to rust.
Joy flows, listening to all birds' choirs.
Cast in beauty's muster.

Basic Colors

Blue, green, tan, colors of the New England coast,
splashes of white shimmer and shine.
Communicants breathe incense of kelp and iodine.
Seagulls bow their heads before they dine.

Splashes of white shimmer and shine
when the sea is sheathed in sapphire blue.
Seagulls bow their heads before they dine,
stand on sacred ground of living stones.

When the sea is sheathed in sapphire blue,
communicants breathe incense of kelp and iodine,
stand on sacred ground of living stones,
blue, green, tan, colors of the New England coast.

Infusion

Hydrangeas bowed their
pink-blue heads when a
snail friend came to call.
The sun shone through
his moonstone shell,
illuminated leaf.
Enter quietly interiority.
Reception is in
Revelation Hall.

Nor'easter

Spelling out
Northeaster:
Wind,
Rain,
Flood tides
Pounding the
New England
Coastline,
Hammering
Inward.

Masked Desire

Sea horses, waves with back-spray manes
blowing in the wind,
gallop towards the finishing line
at the high water mark
finding rest in salt marsh corrals.
Storm after storm, year after year,
decade after decade, generation after generation,
the horses race without regard
for rewards or blue ribbons.
People of the coastline contemplate wild beauty,
the ocean's power to take and give.

Scholars cite the ancient fear
of chaos churning in water deep as
cloud-cast night.
Seers envision mythic heroes
riding pure-white horses.
In the starlight
lone rangers draw their rescue-power,
picturing moonlight brightening,
trust triumphing, peace ascending.

Etheree of Tides

Salt
Tides flow
Higher than
Ocean swells rose
Ten years ago as
If two thousand and eight
Is the latest date to see
That global warming waves Neptune's
Tears as he mourns climate change, charging
Soul mates to arise and speak from sea depths.

Rockport Town Meeting

Town Meeting:
More refined than
Assemblies in ancient
Greece where voting
Was confined to men.

Town Meeting:
Deliberating,
Discussing,
Debating,
(No cussing)
Creating community
By our design.

Town Meeting:
Voting assigned
By inner conscience
Civic duty, courage
To participate.

Town Meeting:
Democracy's sign,
Rooted in the past,
Flying into the future
With hope and freedom
Deeply aligned.

Uncertain Forecast
Counter-melody to William Carlos Williams

Before the storm,
the snow-plow,
in the driveway
next door, with
a yellow scoop
facing the road
waits.
Memories of winters
past drift back.
The future waits.
The plow and that
"red wheelbarrow"
compete.
So much depends
upon the DPW.

Dumpster Divers

Before poet-skaters swirl across white ice,
there is a time of dumpster diving.
Duration.
Duration.
Duration.
Like bouncy box springs
amid coffee grounds and melon rinds
or discarded words from worn lexicons,
sprung rhythms are holy finds.
Skaters twirl like whirling dervishes
in that hallowed place called *dumpster*.

Freebie

In case future
cultural historians
want to know,
Ernie found a book
of postcards with
Frank Lloyd Wright's
architectural drawings
in the Swap Shop at
the Rockport Dump.
(Excuse me, Transfer Station.)
Might as well use them.
Saving and sharing are
support beams of a
recycling design—
assigned by community.

History Lesson

When my friend Cheryl
was a recent graduate of
Forsyth Dental School,
she wrote an article
defending the use of
fluoride in drinking water.
Her grandmother received
a telephone call.
"How long has Cheryl been a Communist?"
We laugh now.
Fear was not funny then.
If we do not remember,
fanaticism could bite again.

Library Trio-let

Card catalog holds all the world,
My high school metanarrative.
Until the Internet, Queen Earl.
Card catalog holds all the world,
Librarians are in a whirl,
Ordering books imperative.
Card catalog holds all the world,
My high school metanarrative.

Library Trio-let 2

Then along came Camilla Ayers
Helping all library patrons.
Learn, not fear computer nightmares.
Then along came Camilla Ayers
For reading life she deeply cares.
New kinds of order, fresh icons—
Then along came Camilla Ayers
Helping all library patrons.

For John Ronan
April, 2014

There could be
worse things than
dying while writing
a sonnet:
singing of sex
or sighting of God,
whatsoever the
affinities of the day
may be.
There could be
worse things than
dying while crafting
a couplet or painting
a poem, or counting
the stars that light
the midnight of
a writing life.

Sky Queens
(under construction)

Giant erector ® set,
red crane against
pewter sky, lifts
eyes to spy hope
in the promise
of power, royal gift
from wind turbines
blowing fresh life
into community.
Sky Queens issue
decrees renewing
the call of the future.

Sky Queens
(constructed)

In postmodernism's
deconstruction,
delft reversed,
white pin-wheels
against blue sky,
proudly proclaim
that a phoenix breeds.
Pieces slowly converge
into a collage formed
in churning chaos.
New constructions
arise, arise, arise,
Green ways will emerge.
Turning, turning, turning.

Holy Hopefulness

Blue and white day:
Winter rose of Sharon branches
bloom with snow puffs.
Cherry blossoms,
against cobalt of noon and navy of night, delight.

Lacey loveliness seeds anticipation of graced greening
when leaves will turn and justice will bend
to the "healing of the nations"
with peace flowing sap from boles of beauty:
treasure trunks of trees and travelers.

Conservation shall cause new buds to swell
then leaf anew.
Journeyers will skip along shared paths to
saving commonwealth.

Art Class Sonnet

Art class the warm summer when I turned nine,
By lovely Evelyn Longley taught.
I rode the bus from Pigeon Cove each time
Favorite days when colors all I sought.
Sunshine, white clouds and Motif # One
Rockport icon drawn, painted carefully.
My word-free, arty world had just begun
Line, love, texture ahead applied fully.
Mixed blue and white made perfect, summer sky
To remember on future, foggy days.
In time, too soon, we had to say *Goodbye*.
Color memories keep sadness at bay.
There is present sense of eternal time.
Art goes on—creative process assigned.

Variations on Motif No. 1

In May, the month
of Motif No.1 Day,
brooding fog
might lift off shore.
Trees are aglow
in the fullness
of peridot.
The happiest green
of the year
announces Spring.
Good cheer appears.
Hope sings.

Poet Reporting
July 11, 2012

Parent swans, bookends holding together
five teenage siblings whose bills have not yet turned to orange,
swim in a line across Back Beach
exploring the world beyond Henry's Pond.

Approaching the shore
they stop at the water's edge,
eating I do not know what fare,
seaweed perhaps.

No camera today,
I must make-do with words;
inadequate but that's not an excuse
for not trying.

A man stands ten feet from the foam line.
The swans float unafraid.
A young woman calmly ventures close.
I am found in wonder.

Sonnet of Faith

Frost is on the pumpkin and the Prius.
Hydrangea blues have turned to pinkish plum.
New England calls the whole world to see us:
Purple asters, white, yellow, orange mums.
Stonewalls, straight paths signal hard knowledge
of coming winter, snow, sleet, graying days.
Stewing time in pots and minds will polish.
Writing song; art seeds thoughts for warming May.
Horizons dimmed by fog and northeast gales,
yet rose-pink and amethyst light the sky.
Take up your best: imagine, forward sail.
Keep on. Persist. Grow strong. Inwardly fly.
Sunlight breaks through. Kiss peace with golden mist
resurrecting courage to bless, then risk.

Advent Waiting

Sunlight shining through scallop shells
glowing on the Christmas tree
creates symbols of sacred journeys
to Wisdom's winning light.

Glowing on the Christmas tree
each ornament hung with hope to turn
to Wisdom's winning light
when darkness will be overcome by goodness.

Each ornament hung with hope to turn
creates symbols of sacred journeys
when darkness will be overcome by goodness.
Sunlight shining through scallop shells.

Christmas Tree Sonnet

When Amy was a Keene State College girl
On route we bought a tiny, blue spruce tree.
Nature adorned with strings of snow-white pearls
Pure loveliness is interpretive key.
The tree grew large and blocked our driveway view.
Cutting it down would be solution sad.
Hugh Collins, arborist, sold tree, hearts glued,
Live Christmas tree elsewhere, a story glad.
Do spruce tree molecules have spirit-soul?
If so this tree has its own inmost glow.
Saving beauty is steeled, inner core goal
Expanding rings in conservation mode.
An environmentalist's hope came true
Gifting promise of power to renew.

Feeding

A flock of robins
swooped down to eat
all the red berries
on a twiggy bush in our neighbor's yard.
As the winter robins
rose to fly away,
I, too, was lifted in sacred seconds
to hold joy
and then let the moment of blessing go,
released to flow into words and memory.

Glossary of Glory
January 24, 2014

Fat robins, the biggest I have ever seen,
visited today.
Basic black hoodies over electric,
orange sweaters fashioned bird puffer coats
in layers of feathered warmth.
Nature's pastoral callers sang against the chill.
Mill the day.
Beauty flies to earth.
Flocks rise.
Glory glowing engages exhalation.

Haiku of Onshore Wind
May, 2011

Dark Wedgewood blue sea
with white surf
breaks on cold sand.
Onshore wind fights spring.

Cloudy Beach Day

Hazy horizon gently
defines blue-gray sky
touching purple-gray
brine.
Then fog fades even
shades of graphite.
Embracing breezes boost
the salt of the sea.
Soft mist gives seaweed
deeper hue. Overcast
matches my inner view.

Fog and fleecy
sweatshirts comfort
those of somber soul
wrapped in love
not seared by sun,
society's idol of
ceaseless demand
for smiley faces
drawn upon sand.

Seven Word Conjuring

"It was a dark and stormy night"
foreshadowed by a monochromatic
sunset: charcoal clouds against
pearl-gray sky.

Summer sleet sliced the darkness
reminding me of my grandmother's
remark that I prefer music in a
minor key.

Lingering grief over the loss of
my mother, she thought.
She did not say that but I knew.

Dead Whale
A Pantoum of 2012

Reverent feelings for the whale
People gathered like a vigil visiting.
Boston to Cogswell path, Pebble Beach,
Cape Hedge.
Skeleton will find final sanctuary in a
New Hampshire museum.

People gathered like a vigil visiting.
The ocean gave him up.
Skeleton will find final sanctuary in a
New Hampshire museum.
Rest as sacred remains renew regard.

The ocean gave him up.
Boston to Cogswell path, Pebble Beach,
Cape Hedge.
Rest as scared remains renew regard
Reverent feelings for the whale.

Summer

Canopy of rose of Sharon,
With music, gift of bees,
Mountains of hydrangea blues,
Blessings for the pleased,
Sunset glow on earth below
Holds and molds receiving souls
On the going, on the way,
Of unfolding day, each day.

Legacy of Good Harbor

When I was eleven, my family bought
a green Nash Rambler station wagon.
Before that milestone, going to Gloucester
was an adventure.

Thus, therefore, and thankfully,
Good Harbor was a beach treat,
the peaceful place of my
second-grade class picnic.

Our teacher, Mrs. Hutchinson,
relaxed and smiling in the warm
sunshine, beamed a happy face,
not noticeable to me before.

Egg salad sandwiches tasted
better than ever in the company
of classmates, bonded in wonder.
Beauty was beatitude infused.

Good Harbor's bridge over the tidal creek
inspired the tiny, arched bridge
I put into the miniature Japanese garden
in fourth grade.

Two years later, a blue glass mirror,
treasure of the fifties, birthed the sapphire
ocean in a tiny seascape of sand, shells,
and stones.

Nature's trinity of water, sand, stones
was prologue to the future, to decades
on Cape Ann and across the Cut on a circular
route to the good harbor of poetry.

Magnification

Christmas 1952:
Forty miles north of Boston,
an eight-year-old girl opens
her present and finds a
microscope promising 100,
200 and 300 powers of
magnification.
She thinks about the thread
and feathers that she will
examine more closely.
She smiles with wonder.

Twenty miles south of Boston,
an eight-year-old boy opens
his present and finds a
microscope assuring 100,
200 and 300 powers of
magnification.
He thinks about the worms and
insect wings that he will
look at more closely.
He smiles with wonder.

Thirteen years later, boy
meets girl at the seminary
on the hill, the institutional
legacy of John Winthrop's
yearning for a *"City upon a Hill."*
Dust covers old prisms.
Ancient lenses break apart as
post modernism encroaches.

Lenses change. Polished
beacons light new paths.
The boy and girl, now a man
and woman, look through
the lens of historical criticism
and see how the situation in life
magnifies the importance of
discovering the original
meanings of sacred texts.
Through the lens of epistemology,
they consider the expanding role
of language, standpoints and
attitudes in ability to learn.

Microscopic glass slides shift.
The lens of love magnifies
new meanings.
Ernie and Sharon smile with
wonder.

Sonnet for Sailors

Arnold B. Willhite veteran mourned,
Pearl Harbor, submarines, saw Treaty signed.
While comrades gave tribute, my idea was born:
a memorial bottle hearts to bind.
"Laura, a message off Cape Ann?" I asked.
"Will be fun. Scotland bound?" Children agreed.
Harbormaster Rosemary joined in task.

Billy Lee offered to take it to sea.
Then United States Navy came to town,
U.S.S. Boone anchored in Sandy Bay.
Commander Evans's crew with plan most sound
launched bottle in Gulf Stream on its wavy way.
Meriden to Rockport, Gulf Stream water,
Scotland's coast through Navy's goodwill porter?

P.S. On May 17, 2008, Andre Azevedo found the bottle while walking on Vila Cha Beach near Vila do Conde, north of Oporto, Portugal. Delfim Trancoso wrote to me on behalf of Andre and friends, who have a favorite scuba diving spot around a sunken WWII German submarine U-1277. The friends wrote a touching letter to Laura. Because they understand submarines and the life that Arnold "Jack" lived, they believe they were meant to find the bottle. Portugal turned out to be a more significant place to beach than Scotland.

Cycle Sonnet and P.S.

I eyed a bike in a good country store,
Though did not need a bike so big and fine.
A purple girl's bike just my size did lure
At the swap shop where frugal people mine.
A kind woman suggested a bike shop
Where old bikes are repaired to ride again.
"Not worth fixing up," was not a huge shock.
"But the bike on the rack we can now mend."
Handles placed on rack bike from bike brought in
Created an excellent bike for me.
Happier still, the tires have blue rims.
Such peaceful colors call forth shining glee.
Life cycles back to the joys of age eight.
Fullness of time: Dwell in wonder. Partake.

P.S. After the fix-up, we found a helmet to match
in the swap shop

Star Peace

Bright Morning Star:
*Whitest white,
holiest hue
in gentle light,
refresh me,
renew me,
inspire walking on,
so when dusk
turns to night,
I will trust
in the dawn
of peace and insight.*

Sharon R. Chace

Seasoning

Sun yellow bursting
into flame, settling
into red embers,
rose hips, like
love growing right,
matures and then
one seaside rose
in December,
silently awaits
the frost in
front of mystery.

September Lift

The September sun shone
on my face. Clouds dabbed
sponge paint on cobalt sky.
Sage leaves in a blue and white
china pot steeped internally.
I sipped a cup of beauty
fragrant as Earl Grey tea.
In a splash of splendor
September revived me.

Onward and Upward

I took a walk
and changed a word
in a poem just begun.
The greatest gift of
time is all work
done before the
setting of the sun.

Cart-wheeling Across the Cut Bridge

Cart-wheeling

Turning cartwheels, gift of imagination,
I claim my image of exploration,
remembering childhood trips
beyond the cut.

Before Route 128 cemented Cape Ann
to towns, cities, and larger worlds
going over the cut bridge was more
than metaphor. After crossing the
Blyman Canal drawbridge,
a trip to Boston took three hours.

Going to the Museum of Science
was a destination event.
Hooty, the museum's first, TV owl,
saw in the dark.
Darkness, fear of the unknown,
ceased to be the enemy.
Construction crowned the day.

After crossing the A. Piatt Andrew Bridge,
it only took an hour and a half
to drive to Belmont to visit relatives.
Never the driver yet already an artist,
I studied shades of purple in distant
trees on the horizons of geography and
of hope.

CART-WHEELING

A 1958 trip to the Boston Public Library
to research medieval times made history
come alive. I played with words,
describing the essence of castles
as "dingy, dark, dirty, and damp."
With Hooty as muse, I was a princess in waiting
for Prince Poetry.

On a trip with my high school art class to
the Isabelle Stewart Gardner Museum,
I contemplated the tapestries. Connection
to women, who centuries ago made the stitches,
evoked consciousness of aesthetic flow.
In time I would stitch together my own
mystic patterns of meanings.

So now I cartwheel, turning and turning,
over and over, with energy and excitement,
from memories and fresh sightings
of canvases beyond Cape Ann, the distant
fixed points that keep me from falling.

Albion Haiku

Golden daffodils
Pushing through purple heather
Albion moment

Bird Call

Northern parula,
a small warbler bird,
wears a blue jacket
with green yoke on back,
golden vest on a white,
dress shirt for formal days
of festive, bird dates.
His mate likes northern
lichen but prefers
Spanish moss down south
for building soft nests.
Now these birds are
worthy of a search
even if it means a
trip off Cape Ann.
What's worth a journey
is an omen; sign
of life unfolding.

Horizons

I knew in my head but not in my heart
that the Atlantic coastline is long.
I knew in my head but not in my heart
that there are warmer waters south of Bar Harbor,
Cape Ann, and even Cape Cod.
I knew in my head but not in my heart
that Rockport is part of a wider world.

I visited Newport and saw
the expanse of Narragansett Bay
and the reach of the Atlantic Ocean
northward and southward and inward
through currents of lighter ocean blue—
cerulean and azure, softening hues.

Both head and heart knew
that Sandy Bay is one golden bead
connected in a necklace of seaports.
I looked out the window on Rhode Island Sound
and took new soundings.

Page Turner
Christmas 2006

811.08, a Dewey decimal number,
angel's note in perfect pitch,
announces the promise of poetry.
Ernest gives me a dust jacketed,
discarded library copy of May Sarton's
As Does New Hampshire.
Her autograph, hidden we think, from
the bookseller is endowment of
surprising joy.

Unlike Eudora Welty who insisted
on conventionally autographing
the title page, Ms. Sarton in a
defining moment signed the
blank half-title page.
Black on white, stark as a crow on
pristine snow, less irritably iconic
yet intently independent in the
spirit of the state's license plate
intoning *Live Free or Die. . .*
May Sarton chose her own page
as does New Hampshire.

Well Worn

Parsonage paint peeling,
white curls wave, splashing
gray driftwood.
A flash of insight—
Up close, a photographer
frames surprising beauty.
Perspective is not always
from a distance.
Memories are.

Observed: Walpole, NH C. 1974
Remembered: Rockport, MA 2010

To Walpole with Love

In the Connecticut River valley,
a town called Walpole
hosts Old Home Days.
Refresh snapshots in mind and memory.

A town called Walpole,
years flee in a flash.
Refresh snapshots in mind and memory,
people with priorities of place.

Years flee in a flash.
Refresh snapshots in mind and memory.
People with priorities of place:
When focus fades, essences endure
in the Connecticut River valley.

A Love Trio-let

In New Hampshire a slice of love,
David said, "Nancy, buy the blouse."
Mud season yields to turtledoves.
In New Hampshire a slice of love,
"You are an angel from above,
Making for us a warm, clean house."
In New Hampshire, a slice of love,
David said, "Nancy, buy the blouse."

Etheree of Meriden Poetry Society

Shell
Poets,
(The now late
Laura Willhite
savored as does
Mario Cavallo),
help me understand childhood
memory of holding my shells
rather than sorting like scientists.
Blessed womb-cased poet pushed me to be born.

Punctuation

Promise is in punctuation.
Too many commas are for
pensive poets what blank,
negative spaces are to artists.
Poets' pauses before clauses, and
painters' margins metering
meandering markings say
rest here, contemplate, breathe,
not as deeply as a Buddhist monk
in meditation nor as piously as
a pilgrim at prayer, yet reverently
taking in sorrow and happiness,
ugliness and beauty, falsehood
and truth until punctures heal
in the quiet of punctuation.
In the beauty of rest there is
Margaret Fuller-like acceptance
of the universe, an exclamatory
yes to life.

Painting Poems

In May 2007, members of the Meriden Poetry Society visited Gallery 53 in Meriden and wrote poems in response to paintings. I wrote two poems based upon "Covered Bridge in Water" by Chien Fei Chiang: (1) Misty Memories and (2) Constant.

Misty Memories

Red covered bridge over frozen waterfall
carries my mind back to New Hampshire.
Memories held in reservoir like the
snow melt behind the dam thaw, trickle,
gathering strength in streaming
memories of generous people with
dignity and grace nourished by the
beauty of place with mist and mountain,
summer gold finches and winter blue jays,
evergreen and delicious deciduous.
Mountains of trodden, ancient, ancestral,
grandfather granite beckon.
Scripture springs.
"I lift up my eyes to the hills—from
where will my help come? My help
comes from the Lord, who made
heaven and earth." Psalm 121:1–2 (NRSV)

Constant

Under the sky there is a red covered bridge.
Under the bridge there is ice.
Under the ice there is water that in time
will evaporate into clouds and return to
the earth as rain.

Under visions of heaven there are
yearnings for covering and connection.
Under the yearnings there is chill.
Under the chill there is eternal flux
energizing continuing creation
flowing into the future.

A Haiku of a Mighty Morning

North woods at sunrise:
purple, yellow, orange, pink,
mountains, mist, moose, Maine.

Spring Trio-let
2011

In Memory of Elizabeth Barnett
Literary Executor (1986–2010)
For Edna St. Vincent Millay

Kettles warm homes in April rain
Promising green in days of May.
All along down-east coast of Maine,
Kettles warm homes in April rain
Melting away icicle canes.
Birds and flowers will sing and sway.
Kettles warm homes in April rain
Promising green in days of May.

Spring Triolet 2011

In Memory of Elizabeth Barnett
Literary Executor [1986-2010]
For Edna St. Vincent Millay

Kettles warm homes in April rain
Promising green in days of May.
All along down-east coast of Maine.
Kettles warm homes in April rain
Melting away icicle canes.
Birds and flowers will sing and sway.
Kettles warm homes in April rain
Promising green in days of May.

Sharon R. Chace

Postcard from Michigan
2009

Hello, Friends,
in New England:
Here in Michigan,
Silver Lake;
dappled dunes,
green splotches
on sand touch
marbled sky,
splashing the water
with sunset light.
Intimations of infinity
lift and linger.
Lovingly,
Sharon

Haiku Trilogy

Zion
Virgin River walk:
Cold water, smooth stones and I
smile from inner life.

North Rim—Grand Canyon
Tears of solemn joy:
Rust and green cliffs plunge into
canyon and my heart.

Bryce
Vermont fall maples
in hoodoos and pinnacles,
deepest turquoise sky.

Plant Life

Sacred datura, white trumpet flowers
call to death or dreams.
Life comes to the chosen ones of ancient
Paiute tribes.
Victory bugles summon other prophets,
from diverse nation of many faces
looking inward to receive visions, dreams of
goodness to be, that, like the white blooms,
blossom in navy night.
Rising with the golden sun,
callings arise to support those who slide,
to strengthen the weary who stumble on paths
to trusting, truest self, to light the way
for all who freeze in the shadows of sin.

Found Poem
United Airlines Flight Attendant
to a Young Family
June 18, 2011

"Take it all in.
Take pictures:
The big trees,
Their smells.
Be careful with
The animals.
Stay together.
Don't get lost."

Yosemite in Haiku Notes
June 2011

Haiku: a small form
to express immensity,
largeness in tiny.

Valley of sunlight,
full waterfalls surge
bright-white, holy light.

White-green leaves on red-
brown bark, Manzanita trees—
dainty memory.

Mariposa Grove:
Sequoias invite soft touch
embracing past time.

High country snow peaks:
sacred space evokes silence,
deepening silence.

Mountain sized granite,
Half Dome—iconic image,
transcendent beauty.

One John Muir book called
The Yosemite like a
lifeboat, saving earth.

A Ghazal Celebrating Elder Men

The Old Man of the Mountain in Franconia Notch, New Hampshire crashed down; thunder reverberating throughout the news.

His passage was marked and mourned, yet his western kin lives high in the Grand Canyon, above the flow of the Colorado River.

On May 16, 2012, not far from the entrance into Lake Mead, I looked up from the river boat and saw Grand Canyon Grand Father.

Memories and present vision evoke trust in transcendent good will, growing into benevolence winning all wars of division.

Someone from New Hampshire must have spotted the ties that bind,
Or maybe not, I have to tell this tale to anyone who will listen.

My hope is to be remembered for my sighting and my sharing.

Sincerely, Sharon R. Chace

Photography credit: Sharon Chace.

Across the Continent

A childhood game drew me beyond Cape Ann.
Cast the dice, connect the dots, push inland.
Busses bend towards future publisher in Oregon,
state name of Pigeon Cove skating pond.

Cast the dice, connect the dots, push inland.
Each player yearns to win safe navigation.
State name of Pigeon Cove skating pond.
Sing with self-understanding on routes ahead.

Each player yearns to win safe navigation.
Busses bend towards future publisher in Oregon.
Sing with self-understanding on routes ahead.
A childhood game drew me beyond Cape Ann.

Japanese Gardens
Portland, Oregon

Water, rocks, plants,
the sacred three of the Japanese Garden
remind me of my childhood, miniature garden
in a round, white bowl.
I am the girl of nine seeing the world in bits of moss.
I am the high school girl with her head in the heavens.
I am the college woman discovering haiku.
I am the young mother walking with my daughter
among the cherry blossoms.
I am a woman of seventy connecting the stepping stones.

The Painted Hills
John Day Fossil Beds
Oregon

Green, gold, pink, sage, olive,
black hash tags, pound signs to wonder
invite me into strength
for the rest of the journey. Gift.

Black hash tags, pound signs to wonder,
vistas of beauty, portals to transcendence
for the rest of the journey gift
streaming, saturated bands of color.

Vistas of beauty, portals to transcendence,
Press the pound key for sustenance.
Streaming, saturated bands of color,
an artist's rock of ages.

Press the pound key for sustenance.
Soft mounds of red and sage are gentle,
an artist's rock of ages.
Infinity is in the now.

Soft mounds of red and sage are gentle,
invite me into strength,
Infinity is in the now.
Green, gold, pink, sage, olive.

Photography credit: Ernest S. Chace.

Photography credit: Sharon Chace.

Blanket of Many Colors

Creating a blanket of many colors,
land and seascapes, portals to transcendence,
woven through my life evoke the power to bless,
restoring my broken self with saving beauty.

Blue, the first and *the first shall be last,*
rises again to anchor me in coastal hues,
the basic northeast colors of tan, green, and blue.

Blue light when I was three graced comfort,
shining through vases on the window sill downstairs
while upstairs Mother was dying from leukemia.

Color was my rock of ages, stony Back Beach an ongoing delight.
Loving Rockport and Rockport rocks, still other colors and other rocks I sought.

The year daughter Amy was eleven, we had a trip of leaven to give us rise.
Ernie, Amy, and I found adventure on an Amtrak train
pushing westward in the setting sun all the way to Arizona.

The Painted Desert glowed with flowing colors,
rust, tan, green.
Brooding storm clouds in the distance cast lavender haze,
gifting a balm of Gilead.

Looking with reverence into the Grand Canyon,
of brown, tan, rust, vermillion cliffs,
eons upon eons, layers upon layers, depth upon depth,
left us speechless in a sacred space.

Fast forward to 2014:

Walking in the Painted Hills,
Ernie and I steeped in beauty,
more intimate majesty than the Grand Canyon,
and deeper colors than the Painted Desert.

Contemplating the Painted Hills felt like wearing a soft fleece.
Streaming saturated bands, of rust, green, gold complimented by blue sky invited me into strength.

Black hash tags on the hills from magnesium deposits
are pound signs to wonder.
Press to connect with sustenance.

Mounds of pink and sage are softer than Oregon's Mount Hood with jagged crown,
even rounder than the worn peaks of the White Mountains in New Hampshire.

The colors of west and of east are woven to fashion a blanket in my imagination, a mode of revelatory beauty.
Wrapped in a soft blanket of many colors, there is gentleness, a rainbow sign that ultimately the universe is friendly.
Infinity is in the now.
Beauty is beatitude.

Photography credit: Sharon Chace.

East-West Ridges

Drawn to the mountains,
Glad to return to the sea,
Pulled westward by the setting sun,
Refreshed again by Eastern green.

Glad to return to the sea,
Mysteries of deep ridges,
Refreshed again by Eastern green,
Remembering the reds of the West.

Mysteries of deep ridges,
Pulled westward by the setting sun,
Remembering the reds of the West,
Drawn to the mountains.

A Cat and a Jesuit

Dappled cat, one
Gerard Manley Hopkins
would have liked if
he liked cats, related as
that cat, *Speckle,* is to
"All things counter, original,
spare, strange; Whatever is
fickle, freckled (who knows
how?)"
Well, that cat is high fashion
now, so who knows, maybe
Hopkins's time will come
around for a second, third or
even fourth go round of
sprung rhythm telescoped
into vibrations echoing
through the cosmos,
pulsing, pulsing, pulsing,
praising.

Tilt-turn Windows

Dei Verbum served as
fulcrum as windows
opened. The updating
Church tilted and turned
towards affirming historical
developments. From pencils,
pens, and final type of scholars,
buoyed by oceanic swells,
writings acknowledging
historical situations of
biblical texts, put modern era,
Catholic biblical scholarship
on the world atlas of thought.
With new maps, charts, logs,
and voyages of peace,
dogmatism receded
like the outgoing tide.
Plow ahead. Sail on Good
Ship with anchor of hope.

Winged Warrior

Northern mockingbird,
white stripes on wings,
military honors for
attacking gulls, flies
with attitude and
altitude, winging
brassy and bold.
This favored bird
twirling and turning,
twitters and twits
of moral necessity,
a just war theory
mocking the world.

Greetings

May each seeker
find a greeter
and with the
passing of the peace
intuit welcome.
At the portal of
the holy, open door
is invitation to
the beauty of holiness,
the beauty of color,
the beauty of light,
the realm of God.

Radiance

Crescent moon and morning star
together shine in inky dark.
"For darkness is as light with thee."
The psalmist speaks in poetry.

Together shine in inky dark
evening and morning merge as one.
The psalmist speaks in poetry.
Transcendence and time intertwine.

Morning and evening merge as one.
"For darkness is as light with thee."
Transcendence and time intertwine
crescent moon and morning star.

Butterflies Braiding

Small, white butterfly
flits from sad, blue violet
to bright, bold tulips.
(Walpole, New Hampshire, 1973)

Small, white butterfly
in New Jersey garden too,
city manse haiku.
(Verona, New Jersey, 1976)

Small, white butterfly
kisses my cheek in blessing
after graveside rite.
(Rockport/Mansfield, Massachusetts, 1980)*

Small, white butterfly
lands on lavender asters,
spiraling haiku.
(Meriden, Connecticut, 2005)

Small, white butterflies
fly among purple asters
happy like Ernie and me.
(Rockport, Massachusetts, 2012)

After the graveside service for Ernie's father, we stopped for a cold drink on the way back to Rockport. The restaurant was full so we took our sodas outside. A small, white butterfly landed on my cheek and stayed there for a minute or two. Thus in that instance the white butterfly was a symbol of small, earthly resurrections and hope for the eternal resurrections.

Epilogue

THIS EPILOGUE IS ABOUT two concentric circles, one inside of the other, that are coming close to full cycle. I do hope that both circles remain open for at least ten more years, but in time both circles will come full cycle. The largest circle is the story of my life. The smaller circle inside of the larger one is my account about being a pen pal with Dr. Martin E. Marty.

I have told the story more than once, including my sharing earlier in this book in "Beauty as Revelation: An Essay of Context," about the death of my mother, Katharine Rogers Parsons, when I was three and a half. Light shining through cobalt blue vases on the windowsill comforted me in a nonverbal parable of grace. However, I have always left out one part of the story. Now, toward the end of my life, the missing piece is significant. So, here goes . . .

I had sewing cards that were pictures on card stock with holes around the edge. Stringing various colored shoelaces through the holes framed the design. I made a card for my mother using all the colors—one color for each two holes. The strings dangled down like a mobile. My grandmother's friend, Katie, took it upstairs to my mother. I heard my mother ask why I had used all the laces. Katie replied, "She wanted to comfort you." In 2008, about fifty years later, when Eleanor C. Parsons, who brought me up, was dying, I gave her a framed laminated copy of a mayflower collage. (The mayflower was paper. No real ones were harmed in the crafting.) She enjoyed it because it reminded her of mayflowers in the Maine woods of her childhood. She kept it by her bed.

Just as I was finishing the prose parts of this book, which are the most difficult sections for me, I watched a segment of *Religion and Ethics Newsweekly* and had an "Ah hah!" moment. The episode featured the end-of-life art by Tobi Kahn. When his mother was dying of pancreatic cancer, she could not stand the scent of flowers. Kahn gave her a collection of his paintings of flowers done in curling lines of white, blue, and green. His art made his mother's end of life beautiful. Beauty at the end of life is the goal of end-of-life art.

EPILOGUE

Convergences of a shared color sense and desire to comfort dying mothers suggested my next work after this book goes to print, and in some ways before its publication. Green and blue are my favorite colors. In the 1980s, Ernie and I took a boat trip out of Gloucester to Provincetown. As we drew away from the coastline, ocean blue topped with tan rocks and deep green foliage, Ernie said to me, "Your kind of blue and green day." Yes. On the way back to Cape Ann, we saw whales. Thank you, Gloucester. This happy day was a foreshadowing because my inner editor stored and remembered it. My interest in theological aesthetics, which includes consideration of beauty, forms my desire to do my version of end-of-life art. I will call end of life art *telos* art, from the New Testament Greek word meaning "complete" or "whole." A line from Ralph Waldo Emerson's poem "Terminus" captures my calling: "Obey the voice at eve obeyed at prime."[1]

The inside circle or account of my pen pal correspondence with Dr. Martin E. Marty is also part of guiding forces that gave me direction after Ernest, daughter Amy, and I returned to Rockport. Returning to Rockport after ten years of parish ministry—when Ernie was pastor of Congregational (UCC) churches in Walpole, New Hampshire, and Verona, New Jersey—was difficult. My family was not religious, but no one could understand why Ernie wanted to work at the Cape Ann Tool Company. Well, that is the place where he found work, thanks to my former high school Sunday school teacher Al Holgerson who believed Ernie when he said he was not afraid to get his hands dirty. So Ernie went from grinding out sermons to grinding out steel. No one, including Al, saw a chance for advancement. But a foreman left unexpectedly and Ernie rose to yellow hard hat. He was a foreman with a pastor's touch, which is so much better than the other way around! Fellow grinders who were Roman Catholics came running to Ernie every time the pope spoke. Waging war on dirt in the church, Ernie moonlighted as custodian of the First Congregational Church in Rockport. In time, the tool company closed and Ernie went on to work for several replacement window manufacturers as a quality control manager and assistant engineer. Sermons from the parish days written on graph paper were a huge clue that his most marketable skill is engineering!

When first returning to Rockport, we did not know that life would work out well. I was sad. My family did not understand the move or my interests in art, religion, and writing. My yearning was to contribute beyond the local church to the ongoing discussion of what it means to be religious.

1. Matthiessen, *The Oxford Book of American Verse*, 112.

EPILOGUE

Strength from desperation, sadness, and not being quite old enough to know better, I wrote to Martin E. Marty and asked him to look at my manuscript of meditations, paired with Ernie's black and white photographs. Thus began our pen-pal correspondence.

On Christmas day in 1980, the wind-chill factor was minus-30. The ocean was much warmer than the air and great puffs of steam covered the sea. The steam froze into millions of crystal stars that drifted through town. People of more than eighty years could not remember such a beautiful sight. As long as memory endures, I will remember the Christmas of the crystal stars with Marty's caring shining in me.

Eventually some of my meditations found their way into a newsletter and a journal of the Unitarian Universalist Christian Fellowship. *Eventually* is the operative word throughout my life. Eventually I went back to graduate school, the Weston Jesuit School of Theology, now School of Theology and Ministry at Boston College. I was a Protestant wildcard with a concentration in biblical studies. Eventually I published titles in the areas of poetry, biblical studies, and theological aesthetics. Eventually Marty's and my exchange of letters would attest to a saying on a plant pot that I bought during our Verona days. The saying, which felt like a promise to me, stated: "All the flowers of tomorrow are in the seeds of today."

At the beginning of our correspondence back in 1980, I sent Marty a collage of blue chicory flowers. My art comforted his first wife, Elsa Marty, as she was recovering from surgery for a brain tumor. A year later, he wrote, "Your blue flower-construct is still mounted to cheer Elsa, but she's now very, very ill." The sewing cards, chicory collage, and other art given away, which are seeds of yesteryear, will bloom in my ongoing art that will comfort people in their last days.

Marty's letters helped sustain me during years of rejected book manuscripts and prevented me from falling through the cracks. His interest in my theological studies added to my confidence in learning. The operative word *eventually* means that success has come late in my life. Yet, at the age of seventy, I am blessed with more work to do. My most difficult challenges with prose words are behind me. The joys of poetry and pure color flow onward and upward.

As a gift to my readers, images in this book are available for your personal use. You may want to give copies of my art to people in hospice care and others who need a card. Just contact me to see color versions of the art. As part of my calling as an artist and writer, I have other images to

EPILOGUE

share with you for non-commercial use. Email me at shrnrchace@aol.com to enquire about my art. I look forward to hearing from you, and, if you wish, learning about you.

Sincerely,

Sharon

Bibliography

Addison, Daniel Dulany. *Lucy Larcom: Life, Letters, and Diary.* Boston: Houghton, Mifflin, 1894.
Bainton, Roland H. *Here I Stand: A Life of Martin Luther.* Nashville: Abington, 1978.
Bloom, Harold. *The Best Poems of the English Language: From Chaucer through Frost.* New York: HarperCollins, 2004.
Beckett, Sister Wendy. *Sister Wendy's Odyssey: A Journey of Artistic Discovery.* New York: Stewart, Tabori & Chang, 1993.
Brooks, Phillip. *Phillips Brooks' Addresses.* New York: Merriam Company, n.d.
Chace, Sharon R. *Images of Light: Ascent to Trust in Triumph.* Eugene, OR: Resource, 2013.
Chace, Sharon R. *Portfolio of Painterly Poems: A Pilgrim's Path to God.* Eugene, OR: Resource, 2006.
Chace, Sharon R. *Protestant Pulse: Heart Hopes for God.* Eugene, OR: Resource, 2009.
Clark, Sarah. *Out of the Fog: Meditations For Believers and Skeptics.* Bloomington, IN: Xlibris, 2007.
Dunaway, John M., and Eric O. Springsted, eds. *The Beauty That Saves: Essays on Aesthetics and Language in Simone Weil.* Macon, GA: Mercer University Press, 1996.
Erkkila, Betty K. *My Little Chickadee: Coming of Age in the 1940s & 1950s Rockport, Massachusetts.* St. Cloud, MN: North Star, 2011.
Farley, Edward. *Faith and Beauty: A Theological Aesthetic.* Burlington, VT: Ashgate, 2001.
González-Andrieu, Cecilia. *Bridge to Wonder: Art as a Gospel of Beauty.* Waco, TX: Baylor University Press, 2012.
Heller, Ena Giurescu, ed. *Reluctant Partners: Art and Religion in Dialogue.* New York: The Gallery at the American Bible Society, 2004.
Heller, Ena Giurescu, ed. *Tobi Kahn: Sacred Spaces for the 21st Century.* New York: Museum of Biblical Art in association with D. Giles, London, 2009.
Kittel, Gerhard, ed. *Theological Dictionary of the New Testament Vol.III.* Translated by Geoffrey Bromiley. Grand Rapids: Eerdmans, 1965.
Klein, Patricia S., ed. *A Year with C. S. Lewis: Daily Readings from His Classic Works.* San Francisco: Harper, 2003.
Larcom, Lucy. *A New England Girlhood: Outlined from Memory.* New York: Houghton Mifflin, 1924.
Larcom, Lucy. *An Idyl of Work.* Boston: J. R. Osgood, 1875.
Larcom, Lucy. *Poems.* Boston: Fields, Osgood, & Co., 1869.
Larcom, Lucy. *The Poetical Works of Lucy Larcom.* Boston: Houghton, Mifflin, 1880.
Larcom, Lucy. *The Unseen Friend.* Boston: Houghton, Mifflin, 1892.
Larcom, Lucy. *Wild Roses of Cape Ann and Other Poems.* Boston: Houghton, Mifflin, 1880.
Marchalonis, Shirley. *The worlds of Lucy Larcom: 1824-1893.* Athens: The University of Georgia Press, 1989.

BIBLIOGRAPHY

F. O. Matthiessen. *The Oxford Book of American Verse*. New York: Oxford University Press, 1950.

Marty, Martin E. *By Way of Response*. Nashville: Abingdon, 1981.

O'Roark, Mary Ann. "A Beautiful Place." *Guideposts* 56, no. 1 (March 2001): 40–45.

Otto, Rudolf. *The Idea of the Holy*. New York: Oxford University Press, 1958.

Parsons, Eleanor C. *Bearskin Neck: Rockport 1743 to 2005*. Rockport, MA: Self Published, 2005.

Parsons, Eleanor C. *Hannah and the Hatchet Gang*. Canaan, NH: Phoenix, 1975.

Parsons, Eleanor C. *Rockport: The Making of a Tourist Treasure*. Rockport, MA: Twin Lights, 1998.

Parsons, Eleanor C. *Thachers: Island of the Twin Lights*. Canaan, NH: Phoenix, 1985.

Parsons, Eleanor C., with Rosemary Lesch and Scott Story. *Harbormasters: Dedicated and Seaworthy*. Rockpor, MAt: Self Published, 2006.

Pine-Coffin, R.S., trans. *Saint Augustine: Confessions*. London: Penguin, 1961.

Shepard, Grace F. *Letters of Lucy Larcom to the Whittiers*. New England Quarterly Volume III, no. 3 [July 1930]: 501–18.

Sherry, Patrick. *Spirit and Beauty: An Introduction to Theological Aesthetics*. London: SCM Press, 2002.

Sollereder, Bethany. "From survival to love." *The Christian Century* 131, 19 (2014) 22–25.

Viladesau, Richard. *Theological Aesthetics: God in Imagination, Beauty, and Art*. New York: Oxford University Press, 1999.

www.ingramcontent.com/pod-product-compliance
Lightning Source LLC
Chambersburg PA
CBHW071441160426
43195CB00013B/1986